Celebrations

Birthday

Denise Jordan

Raintree

www.raintreepublishers.co.uk
Visit our website to find out more information about **Raintree** books.

To order:
 Phone 44 (0) 1865 888112
 Send a fax to 44 (0) 1865 314091
 Visit the Raintree Bookshop at **www.raintreepublishers.co.uk** to browse our
catalogue and order online.

First published in Great Britain by Raintree,
Halley Court, Jordan Hill, Oxford OX2 8EJ,
part of Harcourt Education.
Raintree is a registered trademark of Harcourt
Education Ltd.

Editorial: Jennifer Gillis (HL-US) and Diyan Leake
Design: Sue Emerson (HL-US) and
Michelle Lisseter
Picture Research: Amor Montes de Oca (HL-US)
and Maria Joannou
Production: Lorraine Hicks

Originated by Dot Gradations
Printed and bound in China by South China
Printing Company

ISBN 1 844 21523 7 (hardback)
07 06 05 04 03
10 9 8 7 6 5 4 3 2 1

ISBN 1 844 21528 8 (paperback)
07 06 05 04
10 9 8 7 6 5 4 3 2 1

**British Library Cataloguing in Publication
Data**
Jordan, Denise
Birthday
394.2
A full catalogue record for this book is available
from the British Library.

Acknowledgements
The publishers would like to thank the
following for permission to reproduce
photographs: Age Foto Stock p. **4** (Zave Smith);
Brian Seed pp. **10**, **14**, **20**, back cover (cake);
Corbis/Lee White pp. **12**, **22**, **23** (streamers), **24**,
back cover (streamers); Craig Mitchelldyer p. **13**;
David June p. **15**, Mark Farrell pp. **6**, **19**, **23**
(birth announcement); TRIP/H. Rogers pp. **9**, **16**,
18; Victor Englebert pp. **5**, **8**, **11**, **17**, **21**

Cover photograph of a birthday celebration,
reproduced with permission of Getty Images/Taxi

Every effort has been made to contact copyright
holders of any material reproduced in this
book. Any omissions will be rectified in
subsequent printings if notice is given to
the publishers.

Some words are shown in bold, **like this.** You can find
them in the glossary on page 23.

Contents

What is a birthday?

A birthday is a time to celebrate.

Your birthday is the day you were born.

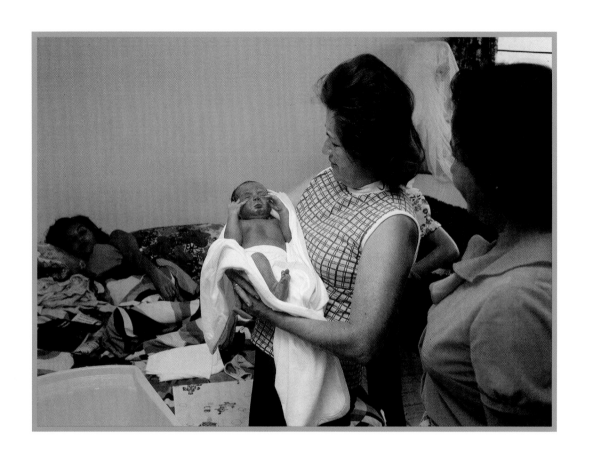

Some people are born in a hospital.

Some people are born at home.

When do people have their birthday?

a
New Baby
Girl

To let you know that
baby _____ Gemma _____
was born on _____ 15 February _____
at _____ 11·30 a.m. _____
weight _____ 7 pounds _____
her happy parents are
_____ Ann and David Jones _____

A birth **announcement** shows the day a person was born.

FEBRUARY

					1	2
3	4	5	6	7	8	9
10	11	12	13	14	15	16
17	18	19	20	21	22	23
24	25	26	27	28		

Every year, their birthday is on that same day.

What do people do on their birthday?

Some people celebrate their birthday with family and friends.

Some people have a party.

Some people go to a special place.

Most people do something fun.

What is a birthday cake like?

A birthday cake has candles on it.

The number of candles shows the person's age.

People make a wish.

Then they blow out the candles
on the cake.

What do birthday decorations look like?

streamers

Some people decorate with balloons and **streamers**.

People can buy birthday **decorations** in stores.

Some families make their own decorations.

They put up signs that say Happy Birthday.

13

What food is there at birthday parties?

Some people eat their favourite food on their birthday.

It might be sandwiches or pizza.

Some people have carrot sticks and satsumas.

Some people have cake and ice cream.

What do people wear at birthday parties?

Some people get new clothes for their birthday.

They might wear something smart or a party dress.

Others wear a T-shirt and jeans.

Some people wear party hats.

What birthday games do children play?

Some children play 'Pin the Tail on the Donkey'.

Some children play 'Pass the Parcel'.

The last child to unwrap the parcel gets the prize.

What do people get on their birthday?

People get cards and presents on their birthday.

Friends may bring presents to a birthday party.

Your birthday is a special day!

Quiz

You might see these things on a birthday.

Can you name them?

Look for the answers on page 24.

? ? ?

Glossary

birth announcement
card saying a new baby has been born

decorations
things put up to make a room look nice

satsuma
a small orange that is easy to peel

streamers
long thin strips of coloured paper used
for decoration

Index

Answers to quiz on page 22

| balloon | sign | streamers |